PRAISE FOR *THE ONWARD SONG*

"I'm spellbound. *The Onward Song* is more than a book, it's a beckoning—sometimes 'a quiet invitation to truly live' and at other times an urgent mandate to ignite, to blaze. I love it. I love these poems: musical, playful and metaphor-rich, equal parts philosophy and quotidian life. I love how they bloom with each reading. I love how they converse across time with artists, poets, thinkers, songs. Wise. Passionate. Restless. Generous. A triumph of a first collection."

—Rosemerry Wahtola Trommer, author of *The Unfolding* and host of *The Poetic Path*

"*The Onward Song* is a gorgeous collection. K.J. Paradis demonstrates his immense command of language as well as an understanding of the human condition—with all its beauty and heartbreak. These poems do what only the best poetry does: it prompts us to look more closely at the smallest details around us and reminds us what it is to be alive."

—Meg Mitchell Moore, author of *Vacationland*

"A riveting, gorgeous collection of poems, *The Onward Song* melds vivid imagery, elegant introspection, and masterful wordplay. K.J. Paradis's delightful debut collection brims with love, passion, and vulnerability. It's a must-read for everyone who seeks beauty through words."

—Megha Sood, author of *My Body Lives Like a Threat*

"Reading K.J. Paradis's *The Onward Song* inspires me. I found myself captivated by the familiarity of "Old Boots," the sensuality of "First Time," the innocence of "Dance Recital At Thirteen," the ethereality of "The Seated Queen," the humor of "A Full Wink Of Semicolons," the poignance of "Eulogy," the hidden wonders of "A Different Prelude," and a glimpse into the poet's private world in "Faint Hope." I'm so glad K.J. Paradis has shared his literary gifts in this delightful collection of poems."

—Tim Hassett-Salley, author of *Strike Two, You're Out* and *Samsara Interrupted*

"In this fine collection, K.J. Paradis tends to melodies both temporal and timeless: spoken on trains, heard in a goldfinch's warble, frost-laced on a casement window. "We linger in moment . . . ," he reminds us, and you will wish to linger in the myriad moments of these poems."

—Jennifer A. Sutherland. author of *Bullet Points*

"Experiencing *The Onward Song* is not just to read poetry but to be entranced by oil-painted landscapes and vivid epiphanies. Deep and rich, these poems remain in your memory long after closing your eyes or setting the collection aside. K.J. Paradis captures your attention and mesmerizes your imagination."

—Maggie Bear, author of *The Owlet & The Cub*

The
Onward
Song

The
Onward
Song

Poems

K.J. PARADIS

y

y

Published by Say Yes Quickly Books
7715 East Highland Avenue
Scottsdale, Arizona USA

Illustrations by Anastasia Yaroshchuk.
Author photograph by Andre Toro.

The Onward Song, Poems / K.J. Paradis
ISBN: 978-1-965342-00-8
First paperback edition.

These poems are dedicated to my wife, Christine,
who continues to inspire me
and who has made all my blessings possible.

They are published on the day of our twenty-fifth
wedding anniversary.

When power leads man toward arrogance,
poetry reminds him of his limitations,

When power narrows the areas of man's concerns,
poetry reminds him of the richness and diversity of his existence.

When power corrupts, poetry cleanses.

John F. Kennedy, at the dedication of
the Robert Frost Library,
Amherst College, October 26, 1963

CONTENTS

PART I

OF PURPOSE

The soul becomes dyed with the color of its thoughts.

Marcus Aurelius Antonius

A DIFFERENT PRELUDE

Why does Wordsworth write so much
about stealing a boat in "The Prelude?"

Richard A. Drosz

I did not belong there—
in that empty house.
Yellow mustard spread thin
on the Wonder white.
A still life in amber kitsch
with deviled ham and
wings only for can openers.

The plastic cat clock
kept its exacting rhythm
in the avocado kitchen.
Eyes in faux rhinestones
shifted stiffly in clicks
as Mr. Rogers spoke to me
in soothing counterpoint.

But the wide river
came without any rhythm
with leaves curling adrift,
riding its attentive hush.
In the buttonbush banks,
the neglected canoe awaited
and beckoned me to journey.

LIKE JAMES JOYCE IN HEAVEN

When you came to this seaside town,
the doting wrens who name and know
each slow-tangled swell of sea roses
never spied a halo around your head.

Your salt-seasoned lean of bungalow
lingered close to the shore for centuries
without any interest in Homer's heroes,
without Ulysses restless under its eaves.

We watched your barefoot mornings
staking the awkward easel in the sand
and smiling beneath the straw brim,
painting a slow pantomime of tide.

The sable-flamed flow of your brush
wild with bliss and sand and breeze;
not the critics haunting your blindness,
not the hollowing within your hunger.

We listened for genius by candlelight
expecting your typewriter's clatter
to rise over the brooding, baritone hum
of some Selectric wading in undertow.

Instead, you sang ballads accompanied
by the off-key, knock-kneed piano
or the heavy-pocked jig of Gramophone
and the easy laughter of your company.

As you boxed up the wings you borrowed,
the heavy slide beneath your bed
sounded like shoreline slaked with tide;
sounded like the deep sigh of letting go.

EMPIRE OF LIGHT

If Magritte came for a late dinner,
he might say that light feeds dark
in roses painted on everyday plates
as we shared a bottle of cabernet.

He might ask us to look even closer
for mysteries within the ordinary,
for twilight's hidden doorways
recasting sky with a single lantern.

He might conjure our feelings
about our last glimpse of mother;
about familiar boots that frighten us
with the mud from our garden.

And the evening would likely end
with a flourish of pipe-smoke taper,
a gentleman's tap on the bowler brim,
and a quiet invitation to truly live.

THE MATCHBOOK

Every act of creation is first an act of destruction.

Pablo Picasso

Each flashpoint and its tiny flame
   unhinges him in smoky brazen.
As his striker scratches scars
   another one in rank is taken.

He knows he's made to ignite,
   as he hollows from within,
and when the newly shorn are done,
   he fears what will become of him.

Made to flare in instant light,
   he cannot be in a shuttered dark.
Torn from within before his end,
   he strives to blaze with every spark.

THE SPHINX'S OTHER RIDDLE

In honor of Montaigne's metaphor
for growing wise and tender with age

At first,
in the light, callow season,
this wheat forsakes the sun.
Heads, so sharp-barbed
in thin but resolute sanctimony,
fail to notice the misting rain.
They stand instead in staunch rank,
a braided chain, long-clanging
and hollow atop the stalks,
brittle-tight without any sway.

But then,
in the ripening afterward,
the grain swells from inside
and frays into a current's hush,
burgeoning deep within.
It opens wide and humble
as pride softens into wisdom.
It lowers its rough, barbed bristle,
unknots with the swollen sun
and loosens itself for harvest.

ARROW

The harmony of the world is a harmony of opposition.

Heraclitus

I am your always onward almost,
before blurred with the next bow song.

I am flight bristling in the quiver's still,
the ravenous thrill in heedless breathing.

I am alive in the trim, taut tension,
deliciously within, drawing back slowly.

I am your always onward almost,
the taste of the chase and the red target.

BECAUSE EINSTEIN'S BRAIN LOOKED JUST LIKE HYDRANGEA, TOO

Einstein's 1905 burst of creativity was astonishing.
He had devised a revolutionary quantum theory of light,
helped prove the existence of atoms . . .
[and] upended the concept of space and time.

Walter Isaacson

We could be emperors of our August afternoon.
We could croon together in Silver Dollar song
in crowns richly attuned to his Endless Summer.

Our heads could be too prodigious for our stems
if bending them comes from swollen curiosity.
Then, we might hum with sticky, delirious bees.

We could sing if we gathered in a garden's choir
and aspired to lilt in this consonance of breeze.
We might inspire ourselves to flower in his 1905.

We could be emperors of our August afternoon.
We could swoon with the true genius of empathy.
We could bloom in a delicate perfume we share.

OLD BOOTS

These are my battered boots
   hard with the brunt of trudging
on pathways muddied and dark
   on days that come begrudging.

These are my battered boots,
   marred by torrents, ignored
for journeys rich with treachery
   for far bramble and petrichor.

These are my battered boots,
   scarred along stitch and seam,
in which I am careless compass
   in which I am wander and gleam.

MY OWN LEFT BANK

*Her writing consists of a rebuilding, an entire new
recasting of life, in the city of words.*

Sherwood Anderson
on Gertrude Stein

In the grand city of her vivid words,
so many feel the rhythm of her skyline,
hear the gas-lamp bliss of boulevards.

But I am here for the missed invitations,
for the brick alleys so acrylic with murals
that smell like new meaning after rain.

I come for a smile in the café window
as she writes on the scarified table
and steeps with her words and her tea.

TICONDEROGA

When freshly sharpened
into a yellow bouquet
your soft pink erasers plink

in a slight, melodic promise
dropping into syllables;
like a marimba Ball jar.

Your red cedar musk,
rich with cumin and nutmeg,
is a floral open of cigar box

or an heirloom hope chest
filled with the grand dowry
of carefully folded prayers.

Your green and gold ferrules
balance a smooth, dark bleed
with a simple invitation

to scribble or craft or crosshatch
the meaning of an afternoon
and delight at its perfection.

NORTH STAR

Courage is the first virtue
that makes all other virtues possible.

Aristotle

Let us lie close to our rapture
and be as ironic and courageous
as careless laughter in wartime.

Let us listen for some reprieve
for the incandescence within us
hidden in tapered sheaves of rain.

Let us believe without catechism
in the North Star-brilliant beauty
written into our dazzling dust.

FINE WORK SWISH

With apologies to
William Carlos Williams and Basho

Now, it is softly arcing
over the morning driveway—
a whirl of loft and revolution.

First, the freckled ball—
a leathered relief in letters and seams,
a whisp off rough fingertips.

Only the feel for lift and angle
without the guidance of equations
twists in a flight almost metaphysical.

Then, silk in blowback snap
a Third-Law tangle with an orange rim,
a tousle of wind, and white triangles.

As it falls, my synapses sing
with the sound of filling its hollow
but never even touching its ring.

THE SECRET GIANT

I was a summer child atop the hillside,
   with a soldier's line of streetlights abuzz—
like a choir of crickets hazy with nightfall
   that cast shadows from behind and above.

Spellbound by dreams since forgotten,
   in constellations awaiting their spin;
I awoke beside a tree I never climbed.
   Afraid to travel dusk, I was quick to begin.

And then, he was flung out across the lie;
   this towering surprise of grand Titan,
a shadow of me cast longer than any possibility,
   so that the dark could no longer frighten.

COAT CHECK AT
A WINTER OPERA

The Muse stopped momentarily
before my dimly lit coat-check closet.
And off his soft, black sleeves,
he dashed winter snow in sparkle.
He was both brilliance and contrast
as he dispatched with his top hat.

I struggled with his heavy overcoat
as it bowed both hanger and rack.
Too slow to make return and plea,
I found only his back filling the window.
His white head tacking earnestly,
searching rows of other appointments.

In his easy glide to the lofty gallery,
he forgot his numbered token.
Behind him, doors in pneumatic hiss
clasped closed in a heavy brass clack.
With the libretto in my bellmen's jacket,
I could not hear the tenor's Italian.

IN THE BOX
(HORIZONTAL) 1962

A possibility for Bernhard's masterpiece

The box has only so much room
to square her ripe, smooth fullness
to block her from light and moment.

Because a portrait must be restless,
she arches her back for context
without any regrets to offer us yet.

And the lines cannot confine her
as she overcomes the opening and
turns toward her own possibilities.

THE HORSEMAN
AND THE HOOVES

Astride the steed in fiery steeplechase,
   with eyes so wide in race toward each crown,
my fear of speed outpaced by passion's chase
   in mad escape from bramble-thicket town.

In stirrups high without the brace of saddle,
   knees against my chest held tight with reins;
I seek to clear each wall as faced with battle
   and find a tranquil sea to stake my claim.

Yet, every gilded trophy falls to waste,
   they bring my face a smile that will not last.
They cannot stave the yearning or its pace
   to have my heartbeat match the hooves so fast.

All things slow down to three-beat canter time
   but I must stay astride the gallop's rhyme.

"THEN, HE SMILED AT ME ..."

With apologies to the Little Drummer Boy

As you are born through blood, so am I.
As you become a child, I become a father.
With my first slow, salty-wide tears,
I taste the spangled-sweet of hallowed love;
dreaming of you opening your eyes to me.

While I wandered far for this moment,
I never knew I'd find my faith in this miracle.
I never knew it would quicken my steps—
the poor boy beating a barreled drum heart
humbled by you and this greater purpose.

SINGING WHEN SIGNING

Why crowd the tiny room above the line
  with its mingy Times New Roman ceiling?
Why be confined by shallow shoulders
  when wild loops inspire your singing?

The trapeze swing brings Big Top stripes,
  gliding in swoops of center-ring purpose.
Why not Hancock the page and its sawdust stage,
  and claim your own ringmaster's circus?

BORDER WALLS

Talking, talking. Spinning a web of words,
pale walls of dreams,
between myself and all I see.

John Gardner

Newspaper clippings
   glued in wire-bound pages,
regrets slowly turned.

Wind howls through walls
   Arizona slats rust high
slicing desert sand.

Somehow smaller still
   each day takes one more smile
as she shrinks even more.

TRINITY

My three children
walk far ahead of me
hands linked together,
happy in late-day sun.

Ponytails and ball caps
turn to see everything.
They are more than three
expressed in each other.

They are some divinity,
some hope for next
that burns alight as
the evening train appears.

EMILY'S METER

You brought me on a Journey
   through serifed garden paths
   delicious with Circumference
and steeped with aftermath.

You sewed your Words together
   slant ink in snagging stitch
   scratched on tiny envelopes
from distant souls you missed.

From the tiny parlor desk
   imagining the World
   dashes chasing shadows
on daring strings of pearls.

Your longing for Forbidden Love
   became a Love for All.
   Your light still Lingers in the Moon
and haunts me with your call.

MACAW
IN THE ZOO AVIARY

The regal, slow-blink macaw
  tilts his monarch's beak,
a rainbow locked in a cage
  so hesitant to speak.

Yet the open sky of night
  invites him to replay
in shrill and flat inflection tone,
  the day voiced in parade.

Jarring throngs of visitors,
  endless pleas for feedings,
wishes hammered in demands,
  a fitful darkness in reading.

A witness to the ugly noise
  and the signal so lost within,
does this macaw feel fearful
  of our desperate chaos din?

LIKE A BANANA

If I am blessed to brown in tender speckles
as I curl around my ever-shrinking shape,
may treacle fill my blunted creases and
become a tawny rich with bruisey sweet.

As I take leave of my tight, crescent yellow,
may I be more fragrant in the blemishes.
Like a day savored in its darkening dusk,
may I be tasted just as I become my tastiest.

CHEROKEE RED

*Wright's fascination with Cherokee Red blossomed
with his seasonal sojourns to the American Southwest
in the winters of his seventies.*

Steve Sikora

Cherokee Red doesn't riot like blood,
or bloom bright in cardinal winter
or strike like chafed ghost pepper.

Instead, it mellows in persimmon,
refines Covered Wagon and Lion's Mane,
reframes Fallingwater with its iron.

It is a simmer of summer's tomatoes,
revealed anew in a decadent bisque,
so savory with fall and all its spices.

Cherokee Red is his vibrant peace—
sunset clay in the cleaved mesa,
fading light finding its last melody.

PART 2

OF PASSION

The role, the rise, the carol, the creating,
My winter world that scarcely breathes that bliss
Now, yields you, with some sighs, our explanation.

Gerard Manley Hopkins

THE SEATED QUEEN

The [Cassiopeia] constellation is most notable because of its W shape, which is said to represent the Queen seated upside down on her throne.

The Guardian

I should, I know, only love the moon
blooming bright in her luminous hum,
wreathing her night in cumulous blue,
soothing me with her effortless song,
illuminating my skin in rhythmic white.

And yet, I miss you and our communion
swooning with the reverence of your sky,
moving with your freckled wake of nebulae,
deepening in wounded maroon and plum,
shimmering with the truth of longing.

So, I must love you too somehow,
whispering to you with centuries of night,
tracing the W and sparkle-strewn you,
yearning to hear breathing within and
losing my conviction to ever look away.

BLOOD ORANGES

Each time I peel
the dimpled sweet
of small, brisk oranges,
I taste our first kisses.
Again and again.

As I breathe in
the citrus-ubiquitous
circumference
sparkling my tongue
and spilling over my hands,
I am lost again in the rapture
of our beginning.

Each synapse swoons
with the sugar-shivered,
dizzy, humming lips
that you gave to me
with the slow, exquisite
surrender of our eyes.

And I linger now,
surrounded by this
pungent tint of haloed mist,
if only to remember
the early madness of
my most delicious

expectations.

FIRST TIME

The wind met us
on an awkward bridge
and swept us together.

It made the river below
into a ravenous cat
with rising crests that lift

in tenuous, stalking shoulders,
moving within the narrows
of hushed syncopation.

Our glances brought us
to a peeling parlor
that sipped in our senses,

scented with drapery scrim
like new clay waiting for us
on the potter's wheel.

And we made reverence
out of exquisite nocturnes
with lilting keys

listening to the sound
of parting lips—
opening for cabernet and kisses.

And then.
Somehow.
You whispered . . .

"Yes."

DANTE, THE WOLF

After two decades of eating like a wolf,
with forks and knives scraping the plates
like an endless insult of riotous claws,
the obese critic finally poisoned himself
before someone else made him bleed.

In all that hatred, no one asked for him.
A thousand dinners facing an empty chair,
ending with him alone in his final silence
choking his wide-mouthed loveseat
like a stiffened gnarl of bloated tongue.

Yet some exquisite wisp of mannequin,
adorned with a velvet dress and pearls
at the perfect center of his trim-tidy room
heard whatever he said just before ending,
heard the hope he must be taking with him.

One thousand shoeboxes surrounded her.
Each one filled with slow, cursive letters
spiced with fountain pen and signet wax;
each one written for "My Dearest Beatrice."
His words wounded with his wishes.

Within the careful crisp of perfect creases,
there were words too beautiful for Keats.
Not in some invitation to her painted eyes,
but to an unrequited truth beyond her gaze.

Perhaps he's finally tasting her lips instead.

PLAYING THE PIANO

At first, I tease a trailing touch
before I lift the curving, midnight hem
in rise from off her smooth knees.

She reclines within her wing chair—
offers her tenuously tempered wilderness;
reveals such anticipation and yearning.

She arch-reclines into a vast divine
and widens into each of her sighs
as I drift within the slow beginning.

With a lightly sugared pique of keys
I begin in slight, ragtime small talk
feeling a lilting melody in my hands.

And soon, I am lost in this rapture,
Building to the thrumming mad expanse
of minor-figured, percussive chords.

And then, I simply play for her
and all along my endless longing for her
and my fingers blur without a thought.

Beyond the felten-synapse hammers
that find each tuned string deep within
I am rewarded with her shiver and song.

It is such a dizzy-tumbled communion
of scale and timbre and reckless flight
as we shake clefs loose from their discipline.

And as we fall into the after-drift of saiety,
we hear the echoes of the final chord
that somehow becomes its own song.

And one I long to play again.

WITNESSES

Let us find each other here
within our own together
along the restless swells
of a river we need not name.

Let us find our wreathing
in the braiding currents
in the confluence of touch
in pique and rain and purpose.

Let us learn to listen closely
beneath its mask of icy still,
for the thrill of the quiet hiss
within witnesses of light snow.

Let us find each other here
amidst the smoothing stones,
with a list of different selves
inside currents of unwinding.

THE ALPINE BUTTERFLY
IN A LOVE TRIANGLE

If the bowline is the king of knots,
then the alpine butterfly must surely be the queen.

Boy Scout Handbook

Her impossible wing always remains
looping high above the two chambers.

Even when pulled in each direction,
she is a knot that will keep her hold.

No matter the tether, tension, or climb,
this queen always carries her crown.

MUSIC BOX DANCERS

Come now and kitchen with me.
  We will cinnamon and sing:
    ribboning like peeling apples
      into rings of three-quarter melody.

Come now and carousel with me.
  We will become the love we bring:
    swinging in the dance made for us,
      winging with waltz and its filagree.

Come now and chime with me.
  We will become our song while spinning,
    winding around this tiny profound,
      dancing in a most delicate beauty.

WILD WINTERBERRIES

This bliss of wild winterberries
in their burst of resplendent red
blush just to tempt my lips.
They beckon for fingertips too—
ripen and rise in swollen surrender,
emerging in the rounded perfection
of December hills in surround.

At times, the yearning is the taste,
only some imagining of fever.
Other times, their sweet cerise
spins into slowly rounded moments
perfect on this Winter's path.
Sometimes, I am invited to wander
off this tempting trail of buttons.

NATURE BOY

For Eden Ahbez and Voltaire's Candide

I have sat hungry at the opulent table
   uneven with leaning and beset with fable.
With linens refined and crisp for the feast,
   hiding a knotty kingdom lying beneath.

Instead, I long for our primrose picnic,
   a blanket in a garden careless and lyric
with incantations of laughter and bloom
   as I partake with you the long afternoon.

MUSTANG

I missed the risk her eyes beheld for me
　　to linger with her scarlet-scented now.
A spring bloom in its season flowering free;
　　delicious kiss of distant, lost somehow.

For then, I only knew the future's speed.
　　Insatiably, my needle-feed was heedless
an engine racing through a dizzied creed,
　　so ravenous, forever-fast, and needless.

Each pause lost to my ever-reckless curve.
　　Each open field never revealed in its time
and every slow meander I had deserved
　　was forsaken for a graveled finish line.

Empty with a memory without thrill;
　　a childhood lost to miles I sentry still.

OCTAVE

The octave is a magnificent story
of a rich journey and a homeward return
found within two, resonant notes.

She is the call of all beauty and surrender,
the familiar slender in both echo and flame.

She is a wide-open sigh of seaside window,
an elegant tide transfixed by long suggestion.

She is a restless journey to a distant whole
and its bold return to her own, original still.

She is the double frequency of true beauty
the miraculous distance that makes it music.

THE DISTANCE FROM SPRING

Winter is here, and you are not.
The cold is unrepentant, too.
Yet, I cannot quite shiver.
I bring only the stark hollow,
when even loss itself forgets
that it was ever ravenous.

At first, I could steal warmth:
from our vibrant quilts
and their patterned memories;
from the shape of my smile
reflected in your sunglasses;
from the bronze-skinned
incandescence of you, reclined,
in the verdant grasses.

Before I found you with him.

But now, I am almost awakened
in a neon and tin boxcar diner
in the flimsy threadbare
of a battered chair.

The only warmth is abstraction:
rows of nylon flowers painted
in dusty, fading pigments;
braces of puffy-chested, vinyl booths;
and the splatter-hissing lift
from a short-order stove.

So, the waitress chews her gum
as impatiently as time itself,
wondering just exactly
what could be wrong with me
because I have nothing to say to her
when she asks what I want.

Nothing even to say to you
as you stare at me across the table
with eyes I cannot bear to notice

anymore.

STABLE GIRL

We shared this shimmer moon.
  And I became—within the night—
the rippled white of coursing stallion
  to chase the might of you tonight.

And you, without the bridle or rein,
  astride the width of our together,
closed your eyes to feel the path
  through shadowed scruffs of heather.

We shared this shimmer moon
  as whispers lengthened into sighs.
We galloped along, sonnet and song
  to glimmer fields where rapture lies.

PILGRIM

You send your tender angels to me.
   Words with only thoughts for wings
      lingering in our own smoky incense.

And I, the broken pilgrim, stay kneeling,
   beneath the plight of new constellations
      making cathedrals out of possibilities.

You send your tender angels to me.
   Rosaries smoothed thin from famine,
      prayers echoed in an impossible nave.

GOLIGHTLY

I have often re-typed
these disjointed lines
in the close company
of clatter and return,
with ink-pungent ribbon
and a skyline fan
of typebars in curve.

By the open window
and its summer stillness,
I have listened
for your song
as if I knew it would come
in the maybe of Moon
in the somehow of River.

And then it came lightly
rising from the fire escape,
hinting at so much hither
that I am almost new,
that I am almost whole,
that I am suddenly afraid

that the cat has no name.

LOVE IN THE TIME
OF INTOLERANCE

For untreatable diseases,
ships once quarantined the ill offshore.
They flew a yellow flag to indicate that
no one else should come aboard.

Perhaps
we should keep sailing
and stay adrift
this lilting, blue meadow
without a destination.

Perhaps
without any love at harbor,
our yellow flag
is meant to keep us safe,
not to warn the others.

Perhaps
the red sky's morning
and its ravening squall
is far easier to quell
than their fetid disease.

HUMMING

My humming
rises
in a succulent slow
and lingers in a
husky brume,
with its thrumming
baritone.

Shamelessly,
its low vibrato
asks you quietly
to shiver, too.

Its summons you
along your
tremolo skin
to shimmer within
your precarious
nape

and offer
just
a gasp
in response.

A FULL WINK OF SEMICOLONS

When you journey across the night
without me in your reach, please
travel with a full wink of semicolons.

May they always remind you of us:
subtle like our typeset and phrases;
light enough to curve ink into wings.

May they keep you horizon-wise:
connecting rhythm with its blink;
tracing the long lashes of meanwhile.

If you are lost, may they guide you;
hesitating at the drop off curbsides;
clicking with arguments of streetlights.

May they deliver you back to me,
immaculately black in their reminder
that what follows each halting pause

is far more invitation than ending.

DOORWAY

You don't have to earn this tranquility.
The swan glides along the water,
and you're just smitten by its beauty . . .
and that's how [Saint-Saens' The Swan] comes across.

Yo-Yo Ma

Instead
of the squeal
of rusted hinges—
of halted keening,
you opened me
with the frequency
in teeming touch.

Instead,
there is only
a wander of cello
and its Saintly Swan
that opened me
to the reverence
of long hallway.

FIELDGLOW

The sun ascends the morning trees
   in a stately procession of touches.
It warms the hazy, fieldglow lea
   in rippled reach of blushing rushes.

Through the barn to braying horses
   who scratch its rays with hooves,
this sun alights on the threshing hay
   and spurs dancing dust to move.

Like a groom at the pathway's altar
   this blessing of beauty still stuns
this kindled return on skin that yearns
   with a cursive invitation to become.

LA PETITE MORT

We do not yearn yet.
We linger in moment.
A twilight distilled.

We savor stillness;
a slight mischief of after,
a drowsy steeple's bell.

We now know solemn.
We know frizzle sand
and salt-glimmered shore.

STEEP

This scald of tea
must truly steep,
not cool or retreat
or wisp into fade.

Instead,
each layered leaf
needs spicy divine
and rounded cup.

This drifty spin
of dizzy confluence
needs languid heat,
needs time and wish

before it rhymes
along our tongues,
before it can become
our truly tea.

So I wait.
And wait.
So very
patiently.

PART 3

OF VULNERABILITY

It's only in uncertainty that we're naked and alive.

Peter Gabriel

THE TOURNESOLS

Now that I hope to live with Gauguin in a studio of our own,
I want to make decorations for the studio.
Nothing but big flowers.

Vincent van Gogh

I still see you so apparition thin
pinned within the opened green door,
arranging the brazen, riotous blooms.

Just like you, those sunflowers were
too brash to invite any small talk,
too distracted to notice any arrival.

And I still remember today
how effortlessly you painted them for me.
Just something for over my bed.

Just something that recasts beauty
in scratches of crusted brushes
flourished too quickly to clean.

They were impatiently dressed, too.
Rough-hewn and crossed-hatched
in the bronzy black, wide-open center.

They were endlessly edged textures
that somehow sang in every yellow
and echoed with the studio walls.

I still hear your aimless whistle,
a broken song from some far away
as you waited for me, for a beginning.

Oblivious to the bold redemption
already tilted toward you on the easel,
blind to the flowering deep within.

I failed you instead.
I turned away from tenderness.
With my envy and madness,

I made you doubt and made you fade
like the regrets of late summer.
I spoiled the only spring we had.

WINTER NIGHT

The figure a poem makes.
It begins in delight and ends in wisdom.

Robert Frost

When the moon is this full
and the winter sky is this clear
and laced with an icy wind,
only mischief can follow.

When frosty sparkles round
into brilliant casement necklaces
backlight by our porch lantern,
chance conspires with beauty.

When the tryst of shadows
fall into the kitchen with prisms
that pierce the farmhouse glass,
how could I possibly fall asleep?

Why move from this chair,
knowing that the coming dawn
will tidy these blithe coincidences
into a stammer of stark oblivion.

MORNING HAIKU
FROM THE PASSING TRAIN

From Hopper's window
  she stares out without looking—
pallid, empty cup.

The long line of cars
  jammed with silent, fallen heads
but one woman sings.

Around round table
  enjoying smiles for breakfast
glowing campfire.

She stares at her flaws
  eyeliner lean to mirror
keeps her from seeing.

Bare bulb witness still
  to angry cell-phone screaming
watching madness spark.

Slight boy dreaming big
  to buy small school bus reprieve
wishing to fly away.

THE CARPENTER

You never stopped or flinched
as you cut right through us
with the bucking circular saw
and its angry, rusted teeth
stained with Skoal and whiskey
as you leaned close to keep at it.

You spilled our cinnamon dust
as you sliced our veins open;
oblivious to any of our scents.
Instead, you measured more cuts.
Such stark, unforgiving angles.
Rage hidden in righteousness.

You bruised us all with the heft
of your sharp, shaving plane—
colloping us in an excruciating wake
of sharp, splintered ribbons.
We were left in long, angular curls
to crack beneath your boots.

BEACH HOUSE

Bowing, heavy, ripe
  sea roses poised for blooming
pink hope in famine sands.

River birches shed
  stripped in curls by steady winds
bark sheets become wings.

Squirrels' clatter race—
  a rooftop peak to scale, but
to frolic, not fall.

Sweet dusk sand dollar
  white star center stitching holes
binding beyond boundary.

DANCE RECITAL AT THIRTEEN

*Let go of your daughter with grace, and you'll find her
calling on you with joy.*

Cheryl Barker

Sometimes, you twist as if you know—
as if the heedless tryst and confluence
of all beginnings and braiding and bliss
have already whispered their awakenings.
With fingertips in curved lift like amaryllis,
you glide like spring and all its promises—
from the so slender wrists of this dance,
from the sweet amiss of your becoming.

FAINT HOPE

Everything you love will probably be lost,
but in the end, love will return in another way.

Franz Kafka

The hidden lilies-of-the-valley
still find purpose in their shade,
still find ringing in their tiny bells.

Listen for their tender white:
tolling the quickening of your heart,
slightly sweet in woodland green.

EULOGY

You left me as roughly cleaved open
as any fallen crush of broken stone,
flinty veins spilling only rough powder.

A coffin reflected round in high polish,
I fell into the hushed surround, too,
spinning in the adrift of your ending.

Only in the barefoot devotion of always;
only after years of quiet shoreline
did you speak to me with my own tears.

THE EXPANSIVE MEANING OF SLIGHT CONTEXT

Tiny stems of neglect—
  a bouquet of small losses
thin in full love's vase

People lost in rain—
  huddle tight together but
still remain alone.

The harbor engine
  sputter fails to foreshadow
sailboat speed at sea.

Doll eyes—sewn blue thread—
  somehow warm with tenderness
from my daughter's heart

The Norway spruce
  dead with inner branches gnarl
thrives in fringed green.

The boy who stumbles
  in cruel fields with muddy cleats
sings with a pencil.

DIVORCE AND THE LOST VICTORIAN

Abandoned houses stand empty, foreboding for a decade
or so, but if they are left for longer than that, they begin anew . . .

Hiromi Kawakami

Once, there was a welcoming gate,
passage between the chisel-hewn posts.
Once, they made a widening embrace
with lilacs within for elegant framing.

Now, leaning away from each other,
the posts have matching wounds;
raw granite sockets spilling powder
where once they held strong iron hinges.

Now, thickets of bristly oxtongue
are all that keeps them from a final fall,
unable to enclose within and inside,
snarled in weedy grievances of afterward.

Now, the pock-pitted chimney remains
to rise with its charred, knobby climb
wrapped in vines of wisteria flourishes
that strive to begin anew with beauty.

KOTO SONG @ 3:01

"Koto Song" is Brubeck's delicate masterwork.

Thomas Cunniffe

The cherry blossoms only open
because of their glorious fragility

in their tender flourish of pink,
in this festival of scant hours.

They change the feeling of spring
revealing the reward of opening,

chromatic in each tender lilting
vulnerable even within the rhyme.

And the goldfinch honors sakura
emerging in song from hiding;

it lingers on the slender branches
as every filament becomes lyrical.

Here, the beauty is almost unkind
with its presage of pallid and loss.

Such it is with the quiet ending;
fading just as it all begins to bloom.

APPLE OF MY EYE

Keep me as the apple of the eye,
hide me under the shadow of thy wings . . .

Psalm 17:8

In his ninth year,
he does not seem to cry anymore
when he tumbles far
from the rough, choired heights
of the rusted jungle gym
before an audience in knit beanies.

His eyes no longer ask for me.
Or the shadow underneath wings.
Instead, he rolls awkwardly
after a rough bounce.
Instead, a cautious laugh
tumbles within the rolling.

He is now a luminous round
of dappled honeycrisp
falling alone to part the fragrant,
newly shorn lie of autumn ryegrass
with a more complex scent
of ripened sweetness.

But, if you look closely,
the wound is still obvious.
The softened circumference,
the slightly less rounded-ness,
is as close to the skin
as it is tacit to the touch.

You need not peel anything
to know a bit of his tenderness
has browned into bruises
that will take to lingering.
You need not be his father
to mourn the end of his boyhood
for both of us.

NOT SO CLOSE

Doppler Effect: an increase (or decrease) in the frequency of sound, light, or other waves as the source and observer move toward (or away from) each other.

Oxford English Dictionary

Somehow, it is too loud for kindness
as you climb the brownstone stairs
and pass me without any recognition
that our pre-war doors face each other.

As our street shrieks in shrill sirens,
entangled in knots of Doppler horns,
it is sharp with squeals and impatience
and the rancor of battered, yellow cabs.

You turn your eyes as I speak to you,
as your laughter trails off on the phone,
lithe like the long litany of your scarf,
distant like the hope I might know you.

I am only a plastic black Dymo label,
an angular name in the brassy callbox.
Close enough that you might even pause
if it were to appear in the obituaries.

SECONDHAND

Her own thoughts and reflections were habitually
her best companions.

Jane Austen

Sometimes, they share their story
in the unexpected confessional
with a stranger they will not know
on the long meditation of train.

Sometimes, they hide in families,
offer only a secondhand intimacy.
Holiday uncles who rarely visit
feeling misplaced in the festive den.

Sometimes, they stand as sentries
in drapes that frame the balcony
searching for the playful families,
listening for the laughter in belonging.

Sometimes, we are orphaned, too.
A snow violet so bright with shiver.
A cardinal that trills to herald spring
and lingers by the open garden gate.

HAIKU ABOUT DISTANCE

Road-signs' angry dangle
  pennies clatter into cups
salesmen pay their toll

A circle of fifths
  sharp ring around his mattress
like a shattered crown

Sacred whisper voice
  narrates photo album leaves
both crack while turning

Campfire smoke strong
  in your flannel nightgown folds
burned long before me

The tiny haiku
  leaning into the shoreline
adrift with almost

BELONGING

I hold this word as sweetly scented bloom,
as lithe berceuse of distant muses' weaving
fills winding rills like still, reflected moon—
a raptured song I long to fill with meaning.

I feel it weave a woven wreath of whole,
a flame that claims its inner, empty hollow,
an incandescent ring that warms its soul.
With the voices' homeward call, I follow.

Yet chains of gallowed ghosts' clang in my ear,
their clatter cracks the choirs' rusted key;
to strain the sweet refrain once heard so near
'til *longing* seems the only song I'll *be*.

And as I seek a home still steeped in splendor,
I hope to find someone who will remember.

DIATRIBE

Let all bitterness, wrath, anger, clamor, and
evil speaking be put away from you.
And be kind to one another, tenderhearted,
forgiving one another . . .

Saint Paul the Apostle

These dandelion greens are bitter.
No cleansing or reward in their fate.
Nothing to consider but violence
in the suffering of this acerbic chew.

These dandelion greens are bitter.
These words meant to cut and scrape
do not deliver a wine we can taste
in the grind of some plastic chalice.

These dandelion greens are bitter.
And nothing good can come from hate—
from scissors sharp for this harvest
in the reverent presumption of rows.

REPRIEVE

The late September day had stolen
the slow swelter of high, summer sun.
So, we swam joyously together
with a slight reprieve of season.

We basked in an easy aimlessness
of listless turquoise in shimmer.
We sang with each slight wake as
floating leaves garlanded the swells.

So, I cherished this afternoon,
knowing autumn was soon at its purpose.
One more moment with you as a child
before our rooms lose your slippers' shuffle,

As ever a father, I have learned to smile
with tears I have learned to cherish, too.
Today, you were still the brazen girl
watching me still strive for becoming,

despite tomorrow's looming chill.

MEDICATION AND
ITS MARIONETTE

I know my own lethargy.
I know my awkward hang
when put away after the show.

I know my own tangle,
my heavy-shackled empty
when loathing finds a mirror.

Without a whimper,
I cannot rise.
I cannot become.

But I dream from the hook.
Sometimes,
I imagine gathering up
all my tiny, tepid hollows
and slackened strings of me.
I imagine a little dancing
with a less monstrous stiff.
Maybe trace a better shape?
Maybe show a painted smile?

But I cannot lift my head
from looking at the floor
that I cannot even fall toward.
And I suffer these yearnings
because without them
there is nothing
but wire and wood
and the burden of feelings
that never seem to move.

THE POSSIBILITIES OF MOVEMENT

With the birth of kinetic art, artists were
fascinated by the possibilities of movement in art
and the potential to create interactive relationships.

Selin Ozasik

Wind tugs strong on line
　　asks me to come alongside
in long, endless flight

Bluster, wind-arc turning
　　flamenco heels blur-burning
flame-shaped tremolo.

Lifted off the sand
　　wild-hearted sixes coursing
a crucible sky.

Wings ripple downward—
　　threatened candle flickers
with a doorway draft.

Minting soft footprints
　　curving heels' backward journey
drifting sway away.

OVERHEAD

Am I just the long, repeating slack
of the black, low-slung power lines
strung above the gravel of wrong turns?

Am I just that rise-and-fall reflected
on a curved window in two-step song
as you are lulled into dreamless sleep?

Am I just the deep unspooling
hung along the roadway's thrum
over miles that come without postcards?

BETWEEN TIME

Night blooms with pin-lights—
  grandeur spin to listen in
to quiet breathing.

In the blind man's dawn
  touching Morning Glory bloom
to see the sunrise.

Falling, fragile folds
  drift with autumn's wrinkled golds.
Blithe sweetness leaves alone.

THE LITTLE CHAPEL
TOO FAR FROM TOWN

I am always your quiet invitation,
like a white, woodland chapel
with a habit of heavy oak doors
and a slight tilt of peeling steeple.

I gather into a pride of rafters
still stretching wide in proud oak,
reverberant with our sacred songs
lingering through long Sundays.

In the absence of any witnesses,
I listen for whispy vespers of pine,
for the visit from a wayward walk
that brings the voices back to me.

I stand for the sacredness I feel
and all the tenderness it becomes,
straightening myself into taut angles
summoning whatever sum remains.

And each dawn brings its kindness
warming me within from without,
filling my tall windows with stories
of angled light crossing my nave.

ABOUT THE AUTHOR

K.J. Paradis is a lawyer by training, an entrepreneur by avocation, and a reader by necessity. His curiosity sparks everything from the industry-defining innovations in his businesses to his writing's unique, classically inspired voice. A proud father of three young adults, Olivia, Grace & Benjamin, he lives outside his native Boston with his wife of twenty-five years, Christine—his favorite person on the planet—in a town that has been home to many storied writers, philosophers, and revolutionaries. *The Onward Song* is K.J. Paradis's first collection of poetry.